*Understanding the Elements of the Periodic Table*™

# ZIRCONIUM

Greg Roza

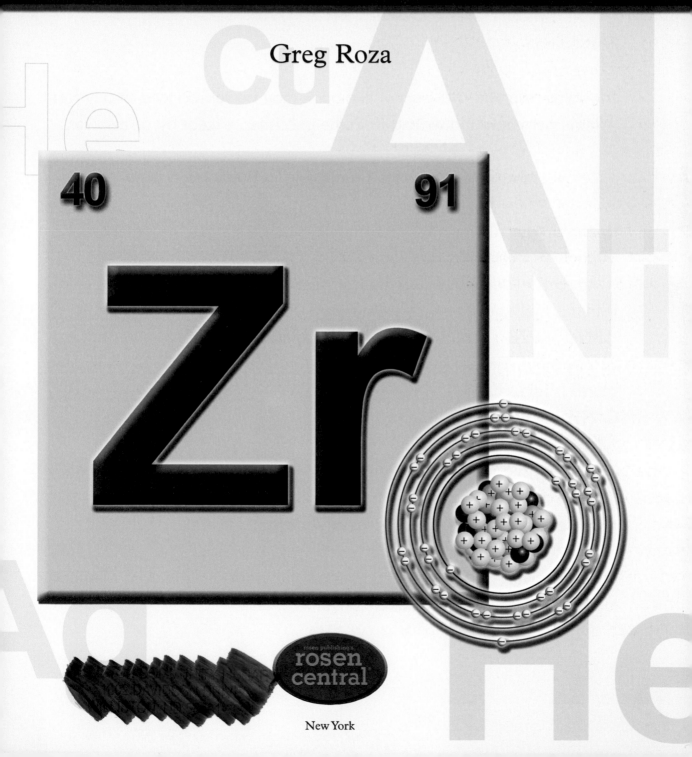

40

91

Zr

rosen publishing's
rosen
central

New York

*For Steve, Heather, Emily, and Amanda*

Published in 2009 by The Rosen Publishing Group, Inc.
29 East 21st Street, New York, NY 10010

First Edition

**Library of Congress Cataloging-in-Publication Data**

Roza, Greg.
Zirconium / Greg Roza. — 1st ed.
    p. cm. — (Understanding the elements of the periodic table)
Includes bibliographical references and index.
ISBN-13: 978-1-4358-5070-5 (library binding)
1. Zirconium—Juvenile literature. 2. Periodic law—Tables—Juvenile literature. I. Title.
QD181.Z7R69 2009
546'.513—dc22

                                                          2008016584

Manufactured in the United States of America

**On the cover:** Zirconium's square on the periodic table of elements. Inset: The atomic structure of zirconium.

# Contents

# Introduction

**H**ave you ever wondered how geologists find out how old rocks are? Geologists can take rocks from Earth's crust and determine approximately how old they are to within a few hundred thousand years. We are talking about rocks that are millions, even billions, of years old. Knowing a rock's age can help scientists learn more about Earth's surface, including how it formed. The element zirconium (chemical symbol: Zr) is one of the most accurate signposts for scientists in determining the age of igneous rocks.

One of the processes scientists use to date minerals is called radiometric dating. Radiometric dating works because of the way radioactive elements decay over periods of time. Radioactive elements decay by giving off very tiny particles and turning into different elements. When scientists know how long it takes for a certain amount of one element to turn into another element, they can estimate the age of a rock containing those two elements. There are several methods of radiometric dating, each based on a different set of chemical elements. You might have heard of radiocarbon dating, which is one of the most commonly used types, but it is seldom used to date rocks. Rocks are too old to be dated by the radiocarbon method.

One of the first methods used to date rocks that are older than one hundred thousand years is called uranium/lead (U/Pb) dating. The element uranium is a relatively abundant, radioactive element in Earth's crust.

Professor Simon Wilde of Curtin University of Technology in Perth, Australia, holds a speck of zircon (embedded in epoxy) that he found in 1984. The zircon is about 4.4 billion years old, making it the oldest piece of Earth ever found!

When uranium decays, it eventually turns into lead. This process is very slow. It takes 4.5 billion years for one half of the uranium in a sample to turn into lead. So, if a rock contains the same amount of uranium as it does lead, then it is about 4.5 billion years old.

You might be wondering how zirconium fits into this process. Zircon ($ZrSiO_4$) is commonly found in volcanic rocks along with uranium. As the uranium forms lead in zircon, the lead distorts the zircon crystal. This can cause the zircon crystal to break, and that allows some of the lead to escape from the rock. If the rock does not contain all the lead formed from the decay of uranium, then the age determined by uranium/lead dating will be wrong.

In 2004, researchers at the University of California, Berkeley, developed a new process for using uranium/lead dating on zircon. The process involves heating zircon crystals to seal their least damaged areas, and then treating the most damaged areas with a strong acid. The sealed areas contain the proper ratio of uranium and lead. The areas treated with acid have had all the uranium and lead removed. The result is a crystal that has the proper uranium/lead ratio. Scientists are therefore able to date zircon-heavy areas with much greater accuracy.

Zircon and other zirconium ores are the preferred choice of scientists when using the uranium/lead dating method. In fact, it is often simply called zircon dating. This is because zircon is a common ingredient in igneous rocks. Zircon is a tough mineral that is not easily altered by erosion and other geological events. Also, it can be easily separated from other minerals that are not as strong.

Improved zircon dating has allowed scientists to more accurately date ancient geological events and mass extinctions. Zircon dating is just one of zirconium's many uses. In this book, we will learn more about this versatile and interesting metal.

# Chapter One
## The History of Zirconium and the Periodic Table

**P**eople have known of and used zirconium-containing minerals for centuries. The earliest known minerals include jargon, jacinth, and hyacinth, which are all forms of zircon, whose chemical name is zirconium silicate ($ZrSiO_4$). The crystals of zircon come in many colors, including green, blue, orange, red, and gold. Ancient cultures, such as the Egyptians and Greeks, used zircon crystals in jewelry. A Hindu legend describes an offering made to an ancient god in the form of a jewel-encrusted tree with green zircon leaves. In the Middle Ages, many people believed zircon aided sleep, promoted riches and wisdom, and warded off evil spirits. Zirconium is also found in nature in the mineral baddeleyite, whose chemical name is zirconium dioxide ($ZrO_2$).

These are zircon crystals as they look when found in Earth's crust.

Zirconium dioxide crystals are often more brilliant than diamond, although they are also more fragile.

German chemist Martin Heinrich Klaproth (1743–1817) discovered the element zirconium in 1789. He made the discovery while studying a sample of zircon from Ceylon, today called Sri Lanka. Although many chemists of the time thought it was a form of alumina, Klaproth suspected that the mineral contained a new element. He was able to extract zirconium dioxide from zircon, but he was unable to remove oxygen (O) from the substance. Still, he recognized that he had discovered a new element.

The element zirconium is named after the mineral in which it was discovered, zircon. The word "zircon" was probably derived from the Persian word *zargun*, which means "golden-colored." Some zircon crystals have a gold color. Klaproth first named the new element *Zirkonerde* (zircon earth, or zirconia). English chemist Sir Humphry Davy (1778–1829) suggested the name zirconium in the early 1800s.

In 1824, Swedish chemist Jöns Jacob Berzelius (1779–1848) became the first person to isolate impure zirconium. He heated a mixture of potassium (K) and potassium zirconium fluoride ($K_2ZrF_6$) in an iron (Fe) tube. Impure zirconium may contain small traces of oxygen, nitrogen (N), or carbon (C). It is a hard and brittle substance, even when 99 percent pure.

Jöns Jacob Berzelius, who isolated impure zirconium, is credited with discovering several elements, including silicon (Si) and thorium (Th).

"Pure" zirconium was not prepared until 1914. However, even this form was just *mostly* pure. Dutch chemists Anton E. Van Arkel (1893–1976) and J. H. de Boer (1899–1971) first produced very pure zirconium metal in 1925. The method they pioneered was used for the first commercial

## Martin Heinrich Klaproth, Discoverer of Zirconium

Martin Heinrich Klaproth was born in Germany on December 1, 1743. Today, he is remembered as the greatest German chemist of his time. In addition to discovering zirconium, he also discovered cerium (Ce) and uranium and rediscovered titanium (Ti). He determined the makeup of several compounds that were previously unknown, including several containing the recently discovered elements chromium (Cr), strontium (Sr), and tellurium (Te).

When Klaproth was a teenager, he studied chemistry and was trained to be a pharmacist's assistant. In 1771, he moved to Berlin, Germany. In 1780, he opened his own pharmacy and continued to study chemistry. In 1810, he became the first professor of chemistry at the newly established University of Berlin. During his life, Klaproth published more than two hundred scientific papers. He died in 1817 at the age of seventy-four.

The renowned German chemist Martin Heinrich Klaproth has a crater on the moon named after him!

production of zirconium. In the 1940s, chemist William Kroll of Luxembourg (1889–1973) developed a cheaper process for producing zirconium. This process, called the Kroll process, is widely used today in the manufacture of high-purity zirconium.

## Zirconium Today

Zirconium minerals are found in Earth's crust all over the world. Large deposits are located in Australia, Brazil, India, South Africa, Sri Lanka, and the United States. Small traces of zirconium are found in the human body, although the element is not necessary for life functions. Nor is it harmful to the body. In fact, zirconium is generally a safe element. It can, however, spontaneously ignite when ground into fine particles, and these particles can irritate the eyes and lungs.

There was very little use for zirconium until the 1940s, when atomic energy became a reality. The metal does not absorb radioactive particles given off by nuclear fuel, which would transform it into a dangerous substance. It is used as a cladding for nuclear fuel rods. Approximately 90 percent of the zirconium produced today is used in nuclear reactors. Other uses include surgical tools and implants, heat-resistant ceramics, and jewelry, to name a few.

## What Is the Periodic Table?

Chemical elements are listed on the periodic table. This is a convenient chart that students and scientists refer to for quick information about the elements. In addition to giving basic information about the elements, the periodic table also emphasizes the connections among the elements.

By the mid-1800s, several scientists had tried to find a way to organize the growing list of known elements. In 1869, Russian chemist Dmitry Mendeleyev (1834–1907) wrote the properties of the sixty elements known at that time on cards and placed them in order of increasing atomic weight. He noticed that elements displayed patterns in characteristics and that the patterns tended to repeat periodically. He lined up the elements in rows and started a new row whenever the characteristics began to repeat. This produced a chart similar to the one we use today, in which elements in each column have similar characteristics. Mendeleyev left gaps in his table where he predicted the discovery of unknown elements, and his predictions have proven to be correct.

# Groups and Periods

Elements of the periodic table are arranged in groups or families (columns) based on their similar physical and chemical properties. There are eighteen groups on the periodic table. The elements of a group have the same number of electrons in their outer energy levels, or electron shells (see chapter two for more information about electrons). They usually share common characteristics. For example, zirconium is in group 4. The other elements in group 4 are titanium (Ti), hafnium (Hf), and rutherfordium (Rf). This group is also called the titanium group because that is the element located at the top of the group. Group 4 elements are all grayish-silver metals with no known biological function.

Each row in the periodic table is called a period. There are seven periods. All elements in a period have the same number of electron shells. However, the farther right an element is located in a period, the more electrons it has in that shell. All periods begin with an alkali metal on the left (one electron in the outer shell)—except for period 1, which begins with the nonmetal hydrogen (H)—and ends with a noble gas on the right (a full outer electron shell). Zirconium is in period 5 on the periodic table. All period 5 elements have five electron shells.

In addition to groups and periods, elements can also be classified into one of three types of matter: metal, nonmetal, or metalloid. Metals make

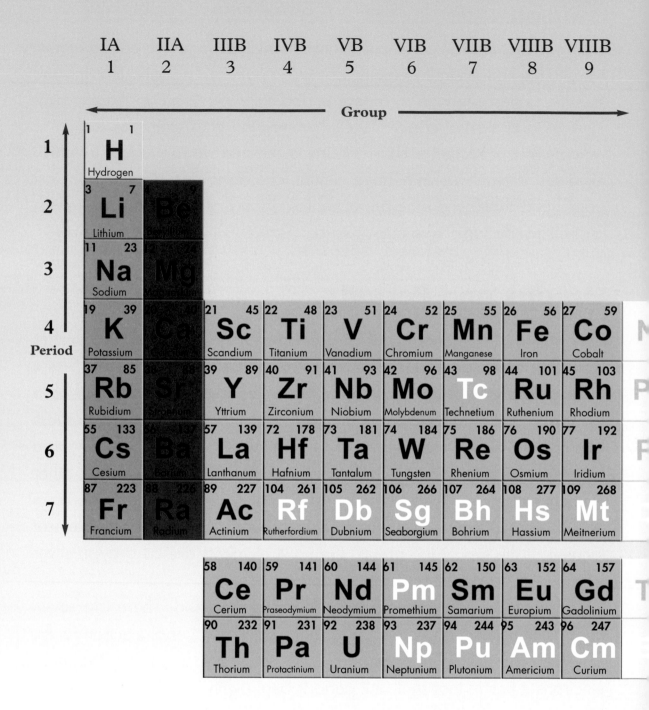

This is the left half of the periodic table. It shows the positions of the groups and periods. Zirconium's square appears in period 5 and group 4, among the transition metals, which are shown as green elements.

This is a small sample of pure zirconium metal. Pure zirconium is difficult to obtain. It was first prepared in its pure form in 1914.

up a majority of the elements and are generally found on the left side and toward the bottom. Nonmetals (except for hydrogen) are located on the right side and toward the top. Metals that are located in the middle—groups 3 through 12—are called the transition metals. Zirconium is a transition metal. Transition metals are called so because they form a transition between the most reactive metals on the left of the table and the nonmetals on the right. The metalloids, which have some properties of metals and others of nonmetals, are located between the metals and nonmetals along a zigzag line.

**P**ure zirconium is a lustrous (shiny) grayish-white metal. It is highly malleable and ductile, which means that it is easily hammered into shapes or drawn into wire without breaking. When zirconium is exposed to air, oxygen quickly bonds with zirconium's surface to form a thin, protective layer of zirconium dioxide. This layer is highly resistant to corrosion from acids, bases, and saltwater. Some zirconium ores form colorful crystals. Zirconium dioxide (also called zirconia) forms transparent crystals that are often used to make jewelry. To better understand zirconium's characteristics, it will help to understand atoms and what makes them act the way they do.

Zircon crystals come in a variety of colors. These gems are from different areas of the world. Yellow, green, and orange zircons come from Sri Lanka, red from Africa, and blue from Cambodia.

This is a representation of an atom of zirconium. The protons and neutrons cling together in the nucleus of the atom. The electrons circle the nucleus in layers that are called shells.

# Atoms and Subatomic Particles

Everything in the universe—including you—is made from tiny pieces of matter called atoms. These are the smallest pieces of an element that can exist by themselves. Atoms, however, are made up of even smaller pieces of matter called subatomic particles. The three most common subatomic particles are protons, neutrons, and electrons. The number and organization of an atom's subatomic particles determine what characteristics it has. Minute changes in the makeup of an atom can affect the way it acts and even the type of substance it makes up.

At the center of an atom is the nucleus, similar to the sun at the center of the solar system. The nucleus is made up of protons and neutrons. Protons are positively charged particles, and neutrons have no electrical charge. Orbiting the nucleus are electrons, which are negatively charged particles. The opposite charges of electrons and protons make them attracted to each other, which helps keep th e atom together. The nucleus is very tiny, and the electrons fill most of the space in an atom. If an atom were as big as a soccer stadium, its nucleus would be about the size of a soccer ball.

Protons and neutrons have almost the same mass. The mass of a single proton or neutron is about one atomic mass unit (amu). So, the mass of an atom is mostly determined by the number of protons and neutrons in its nucleus. The number of protons plus the number of neutrons found in an atom of an element is called its mass number.

Electrons have very little mass compared to protons and neutrons. They orbit the nucleus in various layers or shells depending on how much energy they have. Electrons with less energy orbit in shells closer to the nucleus, and those with more energy orbit farther away. Furthermore, energy levels often contain sublevels, or subshells. A shell contains a group of electrons with similar energy. Each shell has a maximum number of electrons that it can hold. The shell closest to the nucleus never contains more than two electrons. The outermost subshell of any atom never contains more than eight electrons.

The number of protons in an atom is called its atomic number. The atomic number determines what element the atom is. The number of electrons in an atom is equal to the number of protons. However, atoms sometimes lose or gain outer electrons. Sometimes, atoms share electrons, which is how they form bonds between each other. An atom that has lost or gained an electron is called an ion. Ions that contain an extra electron have an overall negative electrical charge and are called anions. Atoms that have lost an electron have an overall positive electrical charge and are called cations.

## Atomic Weight and Isotopes

The weight of an atom is the total weight of the protons, neutrons, and electrons that it contains. Because most of the weight of an atom comes from its protons and neutrons, the weight of an atom in amu can be approximated by adding the number of protons and neutrons in the nucleus.

All atoms of the same element always contain the same number of protons. All zirconium atoms contain forty protons. The number of neutrons, however, may differ. Forms of an element that have differing numbers of neutrons are called isotopes. Zirconium, for example, can have as many as seventy neutrons or as few as thirty-eight neutrons. A zirconium atom with seventy neutrons would have a weight of 110 (seventy neutrons plus

This zirconium medal has been marked with the element's chemical symbol, atomic weight, melting point, and density (the amount of mass an object has in a given volume). Behind it is a manufactured metal bar of zirconium called an ingot.

forty protons), and it would be called zirconium-110. The zirconium isotope with only thirty-eight neutrons is called zirconium-78. An element may have dozens of isotopes. The isotopes of an element are all represented in the same square on the periodic table. In fact, the word "isotope" comes from the Greek words for "in the same place."

Because the isotopes of an element each have a different number of neutrons, their weights are slightly dissimilar. To assign an element a single atomic weight, scientists use an average weight of that element's naturally occurring isotopes. This average atomic weight is the weight that often appears in the top right corner of the element's square on the periodic table. Zirconium's atomic weight is 91.224 amu, which has been rounded to 91 for our periodic table. (See pages 40–41.)

## Zirconium and the Periodic Table

Zirconium's atomic number is 40. That means that an atom of zirconium contains forty protons. It also has forty electrons. Zirconium is a transition metal. Most transition metals have high density and tensile strength. They usually have high melting and boiling points, too.

# Zirconium $_{40}$ $^{91}$ Zr Snapshot

| | |
|---|---|
| Chemical Symbol: | Zr |
| Classification: | Transition metal; titanium family, group 4 |
| Properties: | Hard, shiny, grayish-white metal; malleable, ductile, and resistant to corrosion |
| Discovered By: | Martin Heinrich Klaproth in 1789 |
| Atomic Number: | 40 |
| Atomic Weight: | 91.224 atomic mass units (amu) |
| Protons: | 40 |
| Electrons: | 40 |
| Neutrons: | 50, 54, 52, 51, or 56 (in decreasing order of abundance) |
| State of Matter at 68° Fahrenheit (20° Celsius): | Solid |
| Melting Point: | 3,366°F (1,852°C) |
| Boiling Point: | 7,911°F (4,377°C) |
| Commonly Found: | In Earth's crust in zirconium ores (particularly zircon and baddeleyite |

Zirconium has about thirty-nine isotopes. Five isotopes occur naturally, four of which are stable and one of which is radioactive. Radioactive isotopes—or radioisotopes—decay to form other elements and isotopes. The other isotopes of zirconium are synthetic and radioactive. Zirconium-90 is the most common stable form of zirconium, making up about half of the zirconium found in nature.

## Group 4 Elements

Group 4 elements are silvery, lustrous metals that are easily shaped. Impurities in group 4 metals—particularly oxygen, nitrogen, and carbon—

Shown here are two samples of pure hafnium. By comparing this picture to pictures of pure zirconium in this book, you can see that the two elements look very similar. Because hafnium is almost always found in zirconium ores, separating the two elements is extremely difficult.

cause them to be brittle. Group 4 elements are highly resistant to corrosion because they form a protective oxide layer on their surfaces when exposed to air. They are also considered superior refractory metals, which means that they retain their strength at high temperatures. In powdered form, group 4 elements can spontaneously ignite.

Zirconium and titanium ores are often found mixed in the same deposits. Hafnium and zirconium are very similar, and it is difficult to tell them apart. They are always found mixed in nature, and it is difficult to separate the two elements. The greatest physical difference between the two elements is their density: zirconium is about half as dense as hafnium. The fourth element in group 4 is the synthetic, radioactive element rutherfordium. The most stable isotope of rutherfordium has a half-life of just thirteen hours, which limits the element's usefulness.

# Chapter Three
# Finding Zirconium

**Z**irconium is the nineteenth most abundant element in Earth's crust. Resources of zirconium are plentiful in many places around the world. However, the element is never found pure in nature. It needs to be refined from ores that contain it. Zircon is the most important source of zirconium, although it is also extracted from an ore called baddeleyite. Zircon is found primarily in igneous rocks and in the gravel and sand formed from the erosion of igneous rocks. The majority of zircon used to produce zirconium today comes from sand and gravel deposits in coastal waters. The largest zircon mines are in Australia, South Africa, and the United States. Zircon ores contain silicates, and the silicates must be removed to obtain zirconium

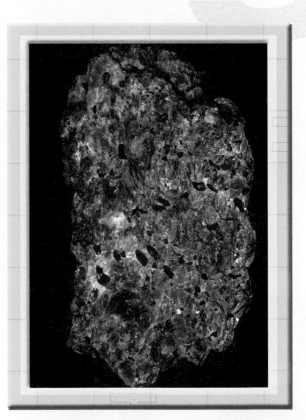

This is what zircon ore (zirconium silicate) looks like before zirconium is extracted from it.

dioxide—the main compound from which zirconium is prepared. Baddeleyite deposits are less common than zircon deposits. Unlike zircon, however, they are almost pure zirconium dioxide. This circumstance means that the process for refining baddeleyite is less difficult.

## Extracting Zirconium

Zircon is usually extracted from the sand of coastal waters using power shovels on barges. In addition to zircon, this sand also contains other substances, such as silicon (Si), magnesium (Mg), and titanium ores. In fact, most zirconium ore is obtained as a by-product of the production of titanium.

Spiral concentrators, like the ones shown here, separate slurry into heavy and light minerals. Zircon and other minerals, like ilmenite and leucoxene, are heavier and more valuable than lighter minerals, such as quartz and feldspar.

The zircon is separated from other ores using a spiral concentrator. The spiral concentrator looks like a tall, coiled (twisting) playground slide. Slurry—a muddy mix of water and ore—is fed into the top of the slide. As gravity pulls the mix down the slide, different ores separate based on their density. Lighter particles move toward the outer edge of the slide, while heavier particles remain closer to the center. The different ores are collected in separate containers at the bottom. Magnetic ores—such as rutile ($TiO_2$)—are then removed using magnetic separators. After the extraction process, zircons with different levels of purity are produced.

It is much easier to separate the zirconium dioxide from baddeleyite. Baddeleyite gravel is collected, crushed, and sifted through different-sized sieves.

## Refining Zirconium

The methods for producing pure zirconium have changed over the years. Pure zirconium was first produced commercially by using the crystal bar process, also called the iodide process. This process is still used today when it is important to remove all traces of oxygen and nitrogen from the metal. Using this process, zirconium ore is heated in a container with a small amount of iodine (I).

A tungsten filament is coated with zirconium crystals after undergoing the crystal bar process.

At about 400° Fahrenheit (200° Celsius), zirconium iodide ($ZrI_4$) gas forms. Impurities like oxygen and nitrogen remain in the solid. A tungsten (W) filament in the vessel is electrically heated to about 2,400°F (1,300°C). The heat causes the zirconium iodide to decompose, and pure zirconium crystals build up on the filament.

## The Kroll Process

Since the 1950s, most zirconium is refined using the Kroll process, or magnesium reduction process. Invented by chemist William Kroll, this process was initially developed as a way to separate titanium from titanium ore. Kroll first used the process with zirconium in 1945. It proved to be cheaper than previous methods. The process has been adapted to other applications, such as in the steel industry, where it is used to remove nitrogen and sulfur (S) from iron, which in turn helps make a superior grade of steel.

In the Kroll process, zirconium dioxide is heated with carbon in an electric furnace. Chlorine ($Cl_2$) gas is then added to the resulting hot mixture. This produces zirconium tetrachloride ($ZrCl_4$) vapor, which is separated from the solid and condensed. This compound is reduced by mixing it with magnesium and heating it at high temperatures in the absence of oxygen. The result is magnesium chloride ($MgCl_2$) and zirconium powder. At this point, the zirconium is mostly pure. Zirconium that is refined using the Kroll process usually contains minute impurities, such as nitrogen and oxygen.

## Zirconium and Hafnium

In nature, zirconium always contains hafnium, typically by about 1 to 3 percent of the zirconium content, sometimes more. These two elements are chemically similar and are difficult to tell apart. Hafnium is usually left in

## Zirconium and Nuclear Power

A large majority of the pure zirconium manufactured each year is used in nuclear reactors. Zirconium alloys are applied as a cladding for the uranium used to make the fuel rods. Zirconium is perfect for use in nuclear reactors for several reasons. First, it does not corrode in water. This is important because the fuel rods in a nuclear reactor are immersed in water. Furthermore, zirconium is not affected by high temperatures. The heat emitted by the nuclear reactions in uranium makes the water boil and creates steam to power steam engines. Zirconium is also a good conductor of heat, transferring heat from the nuclear fuel to the water.

Most important, zirconium does not absorb neutrons emitted by radioactive uranium fuel. The uranium atoms in the fuel are triggered by neutrons to undergo nuclear decay. When they decay, the uranium atoms give off heat and more neutrons. These neutrons trigger more uranium atoms to decay and generate even more heat. Because zirconium does not absorb neutrons, the neutrons are available to generate more heat. The zirconium used in nuclear reactors is an alloy that also contains small amounts of tin (Sn), iron, and chromium (Cr).

A worker in a Russian facility is preparing a large zirconium pipe for use in a nuclear reactor.

the purified zirconium because it has little effect on its performance under normal circumstances. In fact, it may improve zirconium's performance depending on the situation.

Hafnium and zirconium are perhaps the two most difficult elements on the periodic table to separate from each other. Up until the 1940s, zirconium and hafnium were separated using a process known as fractionation. Using this method, a sample of zirconium containing hafnium is heated until it liquefies, then it is allowed to cool slowly. Hafnium has a higher melting point than zirconium, so it solidifies first as the liquid cools. The solid hafnium sinks to the bottom of the heating container, and the zirconium remains on top. The two elements can then be separated. This process must be repeated several times to completely separate the elements.

Today, hafnium is most often removed from zirconium by the process of liquid-liquid solvent extraction. During the production of zirconium by the Kroll process, zirconium tetrachloride is made. The zirconium tetrachloride also contains some hafnium tetrachloride. The mixture of these two compounds is dissolved in a water solution. Then, methyl isobutyl ketone, a liquid that does not dissolve in water, is thoroughly mixed with the solution. The hafnium tetrachloride dissolves in the ketone, and because the ketone does not dissolve in water, it separates from the water, taking the hafnium with it.

# Chapter Four
## Zirconium Compounds and Alloys

A compound is a combination of two or more elements that are chemically bonded to each other. The common types of bonds in chemical compounds are covalent bonds and ionic bonds. A covalent bond forms when atoms share electrons. Because of the negative charge of the shared electrons, they attract the positive nuclei (plural of nucleus) of the atoms that share the electrons. The attraction holds the atoms together. An ionic bond is a bond between an anion (a negative ion) and a cation (a positive ion). These ions form when one or more electrons from one atom are transferred to another atom. The atom that lost the electrons becomes a cation, and the atom that gains electrons becomes an anion. The two ions, because they have opposite charges, attract each other to form a bond.

An alloy is a solid mixture, a solid solution, that contains two or more elements, one of which is a metal. For example, steel is a common alloy of iron and carbon. Steel is much stronger than iron. When chromium (Cr) is added to steel, the result is an alloy called stainless steel. Stainless steel is strong, and it is also corrosion resistant.

## Zircon

Zircon, also called zirconium silicate, is the most common zirconium compound in nature. It can take many different forms. One is the popular

The necklace shown here was made in 1928 and belonged to a prince from India. The thousands of diamonds that once adorned the necklace were lost over the years. The necklace was restored with cubic zirconium gems.

colorless zircon gemstone, which can be cut to look just like diamonds and is often used in jewelry. Zircon also occurs in many other colors as well. It is the densest of all major gemstones. This means that a zircon gem of a specific weight is smaller than other gemstones of the same weight. Zircon is the birthstone of December.

# Zirconium Dioxide

Zirconium dioxide ($ZrO_2$), or zirconia, is a white, crystalline compound. Baddeleyite is a naturally occurring form of zirconia. Zirconium dioxide also forms on the surface of pure zirconium metal when it comes into contact with air. The oxide forms a thin layer that protects the metal from corrosion.

Zirconia has a very high melting point—about 4,900°F (2,700°C). However, when heating zirconia, its zirconium ions and oxide ions rearrange their positions so they are farther apart. Consequently, a sample of the compound actually increases in volume. This results in cracking, so objects made of pure zirconia shatter when heated. To overcome this drawback, zirconia is mixed with other compounds, including magnesium oxide (MgO) and yttrium oxide ($Y_2O_3$). These mixtures create what scientists call stabilized zirconia. The stabilized zirconia can be heated to much higher temperatures without shattering. Stabilized zirconia is a hard, strong compound that can withstand high temperatures and corrosion. These qualities make it a highly desirable material in several industries. Zirconium dioxide ceramics are often used to coat the interior walls of furnaces, jet engines, and diesel engines.

One form of zirconia called cubic zirconia is a popular diamond substitute. When cut and polished, it looks and acts much like a diamond and has been known to fool even expert jewelers. Zirconia is also used to produce knives, scissors, abrasives for grinding wheels, valves, surgical implants, and electronic equipment.

## What Is Cubic Zirconia?

You probably know that diamonds are some of the most expensive and sought-after gems in the world. In the 1960s and early 1970s, however, scientists discovered how to create a diamond substitute out of zirconia. This synthetic gem is called cubic zirconia, or CZ. It has been on the market since 1976.

Could *you* tell the difference between this cubic zirconia gem and a real diamond?

When comparing CZ and a genuine diamond, a CZ gem has several traits that make it a better diamond than diamonds! CZ is a hard gem, but it is not quite as hard as a diamond. CZ gems are brighter, shinier, and clearer than diamonds. These characteristics often make for a more brilliant jewel. However, many jewelers and gem buyers believe CZ gems are so perfect that they look artificial. Diamonds usually have minute cracks and slight discolorations that can be seen when they are inspected carefully with a special magnifying lens called a loupe.

# Zirconium Tungstate

Most materials expand when they are heated. The higher the temperature, the faster the atoms vibrate, and the more space there is between them. This characteristic causes materials to expand as they are heated. A few rare materials, however, contract when they are heated and expand when they are cooled. Scientists call this behavior negative thermal expansion. Water does this between 4°C and 0°C, and so does one form of the radioactive element plutonium (Pu).

Tungsten is a light-gray, very hard metal. Of all the pure metals, it expands the least when heated. Tungsten and its compounds and alloys have many useful applications. The compound zirconium tungstate ($ZrW_2O_8$) exhibits negative thermal expansion. It contracts when heated and expands when cooled. What makes this compound stand out from others that exhibit negative thermal expansion is that it does so over a wide range of temperatures, from −459°F (−273°C) to 1,430°F (777°C), at which temperature the compound breaks down. No other substance is known to exhibit constant negative thermal expansion over such a wide range of temperatures. In addition, zirconium tungstate expands and contracts equally in all directions, which is also rare.

Zirconium tungstate has been the focus of several studies over the past ten years. Presently, there are no established uses for this compound. However, scientists hope to use its unique traits in future applications, such as heat-sensitive devices (thermostats) and fuel cells.

## Zirconium Alloys

An alloy is a mixture of at least one metal and one or more other elements. In an alloy, the individual atoms do not bond together as they do in compounds. The combination of elements in an alloy creates a substance with multiple beneficial properties. Alloys are often stronger than regular metals. They may also have higher melting points, better resistance to corrosion, and increased magnetic ability.

There is a long list of zirconium alloys in use today. They are employed for a variety of purposes depending on the other elements with which they are alloyed. The zirconium used in nuclear power plants is usually alloyed with a small amount of tin to increase its ability to withstand corrosion.

Usually, a metal plate would become dented when a heavy steel ball was dropped on it. However, this plate is an alloy containing zirconium, titanium, nickel, copper, and beryllium (Be). The alloy plate snaps back into shape instead of denting. This trait allows the steel ball to bounce like a rubber ball!

Zirconium-niobium (Nb) alloys are stronger than titanium and have many uses. Some zirconium alloys become magnetic at low temperatures.

One group of zirconium alloys used mainly in the nuclear power industry is named Zircaloy. This alloy was originally composed of pure zirconium mixed with 2.5 percent tin. Today, Zircaloy usually contains other elements, including iron, chromium, nickel (Ni), and niobium. These elements help make zirconium even more effective in resisting corrosion. Zircaloy's weakness is that it easily absorbs hydrogen. Over time, the hydrogen can cause the alloy to become brittle and crack.

**Z**irconium is generally a very safe substance. It is not toxic, and it is not required for life functions. However, some scientists believe that powdered zirconium and zirconium vapors might be carcinogens when they are inhaled. (Carcinogens are chemical compounds that are known to cause cancer.) Powdered zirconium is also highly flammable and, therefore, can ignite spontaneously. Although the majority of zirconium is used in the nuclear industry, it has many other uses in modern society. Some of its uses may surprise you.

## Ceramics

A ceramic is a product that is manufactured from a nonmetallic substance by firing at a very high temperature. Examples of ceramics

This pair of ceramic scissors is coated with a layer of protective zirconium.

include earthenware, porcelain, and brick. The term usually refers to nonmetals, such as materials made from clay. However, there are several other types of ceramics, including those known as refractory ceramics. Refractory ceramics are substances that can withstand high temperatures. Stabilized zirconia is one of the highest-performance refractory ceramic materials, and it is especially useful in applications that involve extremely high temperatures. It is used to coat the interiors of kilns and furnaces, such as those used in the glassmaking and steelmaking industries. Zirconia ceramics are used in the manufacture of laboratory equipment that must withstand high temperatures. They are also used in some jet and diesel engines.

## Zirconia and Portable Electronics

Apple Computers has been at the forefront of personal electronics technology for the past few decades. The iPod has become the most popular MP3 player on the market. The iPhone has also become a remarkably successful product around the world. In 2006, Apple continued its innovative product design by patenting a protective zirconia enclosure for its portable devices. This material will be an improvement over the traditional aluminum enclosure for two reasons. Zirconia is a hard substance. It is expected to resist scratching better than aluminum. Portable electronics tend to get scratched easily from being carried in pockets and purses. In addition, zirconia is a "radio transparent" substance. This means that it will not interfere with radio waves and wireless communication signals, and in some cases it may even improve reception. Whether or not Apple markets products using zirconia, its patent helps show how versatile and effective the use of zirconium compounds can be.

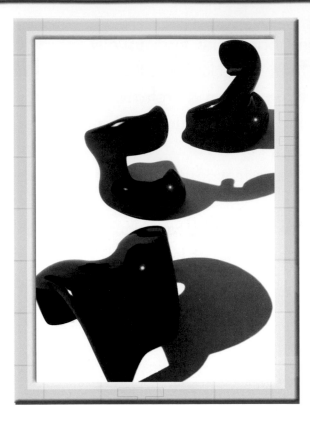

Shown here are examples of Oxinium surgical knee implants, which contain the metal zirconium. Zirconium contributes to Oxinium's strength and durability.

## Medical Uses

Because zirconium is nontoxic and has a high level of corrosion resistance, it is often used to make artificial joints and other implants. A popular knee and hip implant material with the brand name Oxinium has surpassed other implants. Zirconium implants are treated with heat, which causes zirconium dioxide ceramic to form on the surface. The implant is strong, is corrosion resistant, and has a lower friction level than implants made from other materials, such as cobalt (Co) and chromium. Oxinium is designed to last longer and is, therefore, a popular choice for younger people who need a knee implant. Zirconia ceramics are also used to make dental implants and surgical tools.

## Zirconium the Superconductor

In the field of electronics, the term "electrical resistance" describes the extent to which a conductive material resists the electrical current running through it. An electrical current is possible because the electrons in a conductive material are free to flow from one place to another, carrying an electrical current. These moving electrons often collide with vibrating atoms, which causes them to scatter and release heat in the process. The

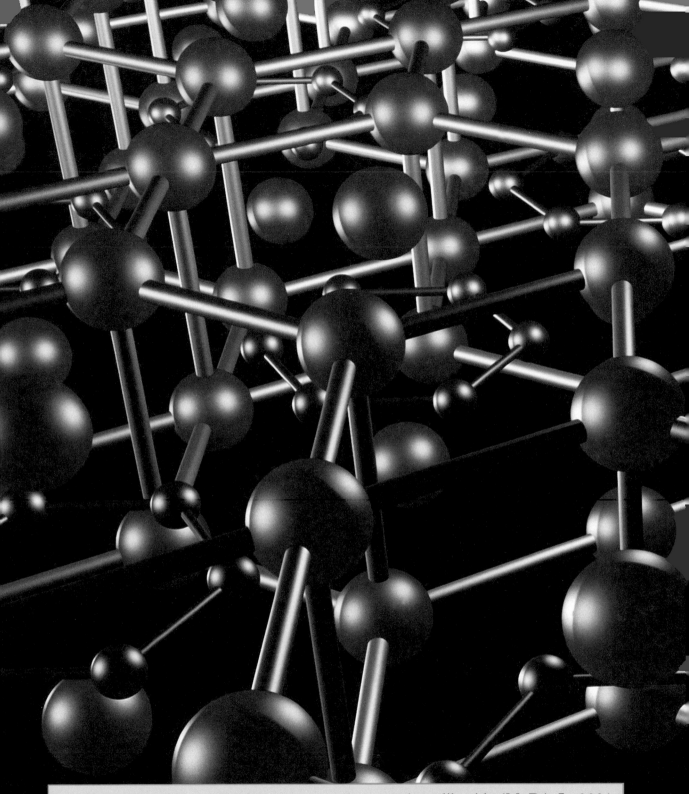

This is a molecular model of the compound magnesium diboride ($MgB_2$). In 2001, Japanese scientists discovered that this compound is an effective superconductor at relatively high temperatures (−234°C). Researchers are also studying the superconductive properties of zirconium alloys.

warmer a material is, the faster its atoms vibrate, and the higher its resistance becomes. Because of electrical resistance, there are limits to how much electricity can be transported by a conductive material.

Many scientists today are exploring materials that have a property called superconductivity. A superconductive material has no resistance to electricity, and therefore, there is no limit to the electricity it can carry. Generally, materials become superconductive only when they are extremely cold. When certain metals and ceramics are cooled to temperatures ranging from about −459°F (−273°C) to −321°F (−196°C), they have little or no electrical resistance. What happens in a material when it becomes superconductive is unknown now, but many scientists are working on

Scientists hope to someday develop commercially viable, zirconium-based super-conductors. They might be used to make magnetically powered train systems, like this magnetic levitation train system in China.

understanding the cause of superconductivity. They are also working to develop many types of superconductors. One of the most important uses of superconductors is in the production of electromagnets, like those that are used in high-speed magnetic levitation trains. When cooled to very low temperatures, zirconium becomes magnetic. Several zirconium alloys are being studied for use in superconducting magnets. These alloys include zirconium-zinc (Zn), zirconium-niobium, and zirconium-tin.

# Getters, Antiperspirants, and More!

Zirconium has many other uses in modern society. Zirconium has been used as a "getter" for many years. A getter is a solid material capable of combining with and removing traces of gases from vacuum tubes. Zirconium alloys are particularly useful getters in certain lamps and photography flashbulbs. Zirconium getters remove gases such as oxygen, nitrogen, and carbon dioxide to ensure the maintenance of a vacuum in bulbs and lamps.

There are many other applications for zirconium. Some antiperspirants contain zirconium in the form of aluminum zirconium chloride complexes. (Some research has shown, though, that zirconium can cause skin rashes when it is used in deodorants.) Zirconium nitride is used to coat drill bits to make them stronger. The compound zirconium carbonate is a component of poison ivy lotion. Think of how different our world would be without the element zirconium.

# The Periodic Table of Elements

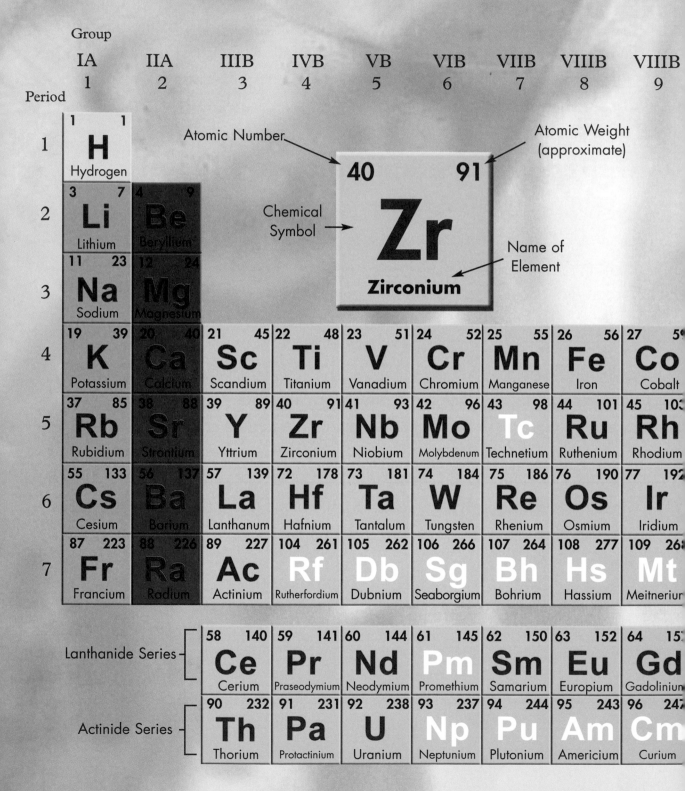

**Group**

| IA 1 | IIA 2 | IIIB 3 | IVB 4 | VB 5 | VIB 6 | VIIB 7 | VIIIB 8 | VIIIB 9 |

**Period**

| | | | | | | | | |
|---|---|---|---|---|---|---|---|---|
| **1 1** H Hydrogen | | | | | | | | |
| **3 7** Li Lithium | **4 9** Be Beryllium | | | | | | | |
| **11 23** Na Sodium | **12 24** Mg Magnesium | | | | | | | |
| **19 39** K Potassium | **20 40** Ca Calcium | **21 45** Sc Scandium | **22 48** Ti Titanium | **23 51** V Vanadium | **24 52** Cr Chromium | **25 55** Mn Manganese | **26 56** Fe Iron | **27 59** Co Cobalt |
| **37 85** Rb Rubidium | **38 88** Sr Strontium | **39 89** Y Yttrium | **40 91** Zr Zirconium | **41 93** Nb Niobium | **42 96** Mo Molybdenum | **43 98** Tc Technetium | **44 101** Ru Ruthenium | **45 103** Rh Rhodium |
| **55 133** Cs Cesium | **56 137** Ba Barium | **57 139** La Lanthanum | **72 178** Hf Hafnium | **73 181** Ta Tantalum | **74 184** W Tungsten | **75 186** Re Rhenium | **76 190** Os Osmium | **77 192** Ir Iridium |
| **87 223** Fr Francium | **88 226** Ra Radium | **89 227** Ac Actinium | **104 261** Rf Rutherfordium | **105 262** Db Dubnium | **106 266** Sg Seaborgium | **107 264** Bh Bohrium | **108 277** Hs Hassium | **109 268** Mt Meitnerium |

Atomic Number

Atomic Weight (approximate)

**40 91**
**Zr**
Chemical Symbol

Name of Element

**Zirconium**

**Lanthanide Series**

| **58 140** Ce Cerium | **59 141** Pr Praseodymium | **60 144** Nd Neodymium | **61 145** Pm Promethium | **62 150** Sm Samarium | **63 152** Eu Europium | **64 157** Gd Gadolinium |

**Actinide Series**

| **90 232** Th Thorium | **91 231** Pa Protactinium | **92 238** U Uranium | **93 237** Np Neptunium | **94 244** Pu Plutonium | **95 243** Am Americium | **96 247** Cm Curium |

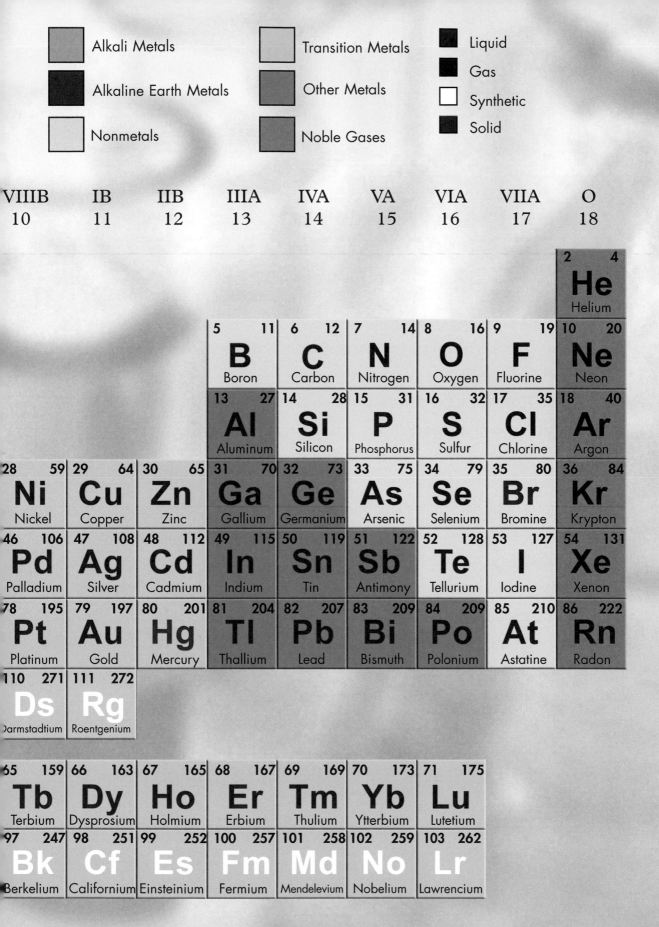

**Legend**

| | |
|---|---|
| Alkali Metals | Transition Metals |
| Alkaline Earth Metals | Other Metals |
| Nonmetals | Noble Gases |

| | |
|---|---|
| Liquid | |
| Gas | |
| Synthetic | |
| Solid | |

| VIIIB 10 | IB 11 | IIB 12 | IIIA 13 | IVA 14 | VA 15 | VIA 16 | VIIA 17 | O 18 |
|---|---|---|---|---|---|---|---|---|

| | | | | | | | | 2  4 **He** Helium |
|---|---|---|---|---|---|---|---|---|
| | | | 5  11 **B** Boron | 6  12 **C** Carbon | 7  14 **N** Nitrogen | 8  16 **O** Oxygen | 9  19 **F** Fluorine | 10  20 **Ne** Neon |
| | | | 13  27 **Al** Aluminum | 14  28 **Si** Silicon | 15  31 **P** Phosphorus | 16  32 **S** Sulfur | 17  35 **Cl** Chlorine | 18  40 **Ar** Argon |
| 28  59 **Ni** Nickel | 29  64 **Cu** Copper | 30  65 **Zn** Zinc | 31  70 **Ga** Gallium | 32  73 **Ge** Germanium | 33  75 **As** Arsenic | 34  79 **Se** Selenium | 35  80 **Br** Bromine | 36  84 **Kr** Krypton |
| 46  106 **Pd** Palladium | 47  108 **Ag** Silver | 48  112 **Cd** Cadmium | 49  115 **In** Indium | 50  119 **Sn** Tin | 51  122 **Sb** Antimony | 52  128 **Te** Tellurium | 53  127 **I** Iodine | 54  131 **Xe** Xenon |
| 78  195 **Pt** Platinum | 79  197 **Au** Gold | 80  201 **Hg** Mercury | 81  204 **Tl** Thallium | 82  207 **Pb** Lead | 83  209 **Bi** Bismuth | 84  209 **Po** Polonium | 85  210 **At** Astatine | 86  222 **Rn** Radon |
| 110  271 **Ds** Darmstadtium | 111  272 **Rg** Roentgenium | | | | | | | |

| 65  159 **Tb** Terbium | 66  163 **Dy** Dysprosium | 67  165 **Ho** Holmium | 68  167 **Er** Erbium | 69  169 **Tm** Thulium | 70  173 **Yb** Ytterbium | 71  175 **Lu** Lutetium |
|---|---|---|---|---|---|---|
| 97  247 **Bk** Berkelium | 98  251 **Cf** Californium | 99  252 **Es** Einsteinium | 100  257 **Fm** Fermium | 101  258 **Md** Mendelevium | 102  259 **No** Nobelium | 103  262 **Lr** Lawrencium |

# Glossary

**control rod**  A rod made of neutron-absorbing material used to control the rate at which nuclear fuel creates energy.

**corrosion**  The process by which a metal is transformed by chemical reaction.

**density**  A measure of mass (g) per unit volume ($cm^3$). To find the density of an object, divide the mass of the object by its volume.

**filament**  A thin wire that glows and gets hot when electricity is passed through it.

**fuel rod**  A metal tube containing radioactive material used to boil water in a nuclear reactor.

**half-life**  The time it takes a radioactive substance to lose half of its radioactivity through decay.

**malleable**  Easily bent or shaped.

**nuclear reactor**  A machine that uses radioactive material to create energy.

**refractory**  Relating to a material that is able to withstand very high temperatures without softening.

**silicate**  A mineral that contains silicon, oxygen, and at least one more element.

**soluble**  Able to be dissolved in another substance.

**solvent**  A substance that dissolves other substances.

**spontaneous**  Occurring unexpectedly, rather than by planning.

**tensile strength**  The greatest lengthwise stress a substance can bear without tearing apart or breaking.

**thermal**  Related to, affected by, or producing heat.

**valence**  The relative capacity of one substance to unite, react, or interact with another substance.

U.S. Geological Survey (USGS)
12201 Sunrise Valley Drive
Reston, VA 20192
(703) 648-4000
Web site http://www.usgs.gov
Created by Congress in 1879, the USGS "collects, monitors, analyzes,
    and provides scientific understanding about natural resource conditions,
    issues, and problems."

Zirconium Research Corporation
P.O. Box 160
Philomath, OR 97370
(541) 967-9005
Web site: http://www.zirconiumresearch.com
The Zirconium Research Corporation produces a wide range of zirconium,
    titanium, and niobium for use in several industries.

## Web Sites

Due to the changing nature of Internet links, Rosen Publishing has
developed an online list of Web sites related to the subject of this book.
This site is updated regularly. Please use this link to access the list:

http://www.rosenlinks.com/uept/zirc

# For Further Reading

Miller, Ron. *The Elements: What You Really Want to Know*. Minneapolis, MN: Twenty-First Century Books, 2006.

Newmark, Ann, and Laura Buller. *Chemistry*. New York, NY: DK Children, 2005.

Oxlade, Chris. *States of Matter* (Chemicals in Action). 2nd ed. Chicago, IL: Heinemann Library, 2007.

Pellant, Chris. *Rocks and Minerals*. New York, NY: Dorling Kindersley, 2002.

Roza, Greg. *Titanium* (Understanding the Elements of the Periodic Table). New York, NY: Rosen Publishing, 2008.

Stwertka, Albert. *A Guide to the Elements*. New York, NY: Oxford University Press, 2002.

Tocci, Salvatore. *The Periodic Table*. New York, NY: Children's Press, 2004.

Watt, Susan. *Zirconium*. New York, NY: Benchmark Books, 2007.

Wiker, Benjamin D. *The Mystery of the Periodic Table*. Bathgate, ND: Bethlehem Books, 2003.

# Bibliography

Apple Insider. "Apple Seeks Patent on Radio-Transparent Zirconia CE Casings." November 30, 2006. Retrieved April 7, 2008 (http://www.appleinsider.com/articles/06/11/30/apple_seeks_patent_on_radio_transparent_zirconia_ce_casings.html).

AZoM—The A to Z of Materials. "Oxinium Oxidized Zirconium Knee Replacements from Smith and Nephew." June 2003. Retrieved April 5, 2008 (http://www.azom.com/Details.asp?ArticleID=2395).

Bonsor, Kevin, and Candice Gibson. "How Diamonds Work." How Stuff Works. Retrieved April 5, 2008 (http://science.howstuffworks.com/diamond8.htm).

Ceram Research. "Zirconia." AZoM—The A to Z of Materials. Retrieved April 5, 2008 (http://www.azom.com/Details.asp?ArticleID=133).

Day, Charles. "Second Material Found That Superconducts in a Ferromagnetic State." *Physics Today*, September 2001. Retrieved April 7, 2008 (http://www.physicstoday.org/pt/vol-54/iss-9/p16.html).

Emsley, John. *Molecules at an Exhibition: The Science of Everyday Life.* London, UK: Oxford University Press, 1999.

Emsley, John. *Nature's Building Blocks: An A–Z Guide to the Elements.* New York, NY: Oxford University Press, 2001.

Greenwood, N. N., and A. Earnshaw. *Chemistry of the Elements.* Oxford, UK: Butterworth-Heinemann, 2001.

Hedrick, James B. "Zirconium." U.S. Geological Survey. Retrieved April 5, 2008 (http://minerals.usgs.gov/minerals/pubs/commodity/zirconium/730798.pdf).

How Products Are Made. "Zirconium." Retrieved April 5, 2008 (http://www.madehow.com/Volume-1/Zirconium.html).

Krebs, Robert E. *The History and Use of Our Earth's Chemical Elements: A Reference Guide.* Westport, CT: Greenwood Press, 1998.

Kubach, Charles. "Spiral Concentrators." Mine-Engineer.com. Retrieved April 5, 2008 (http://www.mine-engineer.com/mining/minproc/spiral.htm).

Rutherford Appleton Library. "Zirconium Tungstate: The Incredible Shrinking Material." *ISIS Faculty Annual Report 1996–1997.* Retrieved April 3, 2008 (http://www.isis.rl.ac.uk/isis97/feature1.pdf).

Sanders, Robert. "Uranium/Lead Dating Provides Most Accurate Date Yet for Earth's Largest Extinction." *UC Berkeley News*, September 16, 2004. Retrieved April 6, 2008 (http://www.berkeley.edu/news/media/releases/2004/09/16_uranium.shtml).

Stanford Materials Corporation. "Applications and Preparations of Zirconia and Stabilized Zirconia Powders." Retrieved April 5, 2008 (http://www.stanfordmaterials.com/zr.html).

University of California-Santa Cruz. "Unusual Material That Contracts When Heated Is Giving Up Its Secrets to Physicists." ScienceDaily.com, November 19, 2004. Retrieved April 4, 2008 (http://www.sciencedaily.com?/releases/2004/11/041119015323.htm).

Van der Krogt, Peter. "Zirconium." Elementymology & Elements Multidict, May 5, 2005. Retrieved March 18, 2008 (http://www.vanderkrogt.net/elements/elem/zr.html).

Wiberg, Egon, and Arnold Frederick Holleman. *Inorganic Chemistry.* Burlington, MA: Elsevier Science & Technology Publishing, 2001.

## About the Author

Greg Roza has written and edited educational materials for children for the past eight years. Roza has long had an interest in scientific topics and spends much of his spare time tinkering with machines around the house. He lives in Hamburg, New York, with his wife, Abigail, and his three children, Autumn, Lincoln, and Daisy.

## Photo Credits

Cover, pp. 1, 12, 15, 40–41 by Tahara Anderson; p. 5 © AP Images; p. 7 krtphotoslive/Newscom; p. 8 © Photo12 - Elk-Opid/The Image Works; pp. 9, 34 © SSPL/The Image Works; p. 13 Al Fenn/Time & Life Pictures/Getty Images; p. 14 © Joel Arem/Photo Researchers, Inc.; p. 17 © Charles D. Winters/Photo Researchers, Inc.; p. 19 © Russ Lappa/Photo Researchers, Inc.; p. 21 © L. S. Stepanowicz/Visuals Unlimited; p. 22 Courtesy Iluka Resources Limited; p. 23 © Ken Lucas/Visuals Unlimited; p. 25 tassphotoslive/Newscom; p. 28 Lluis Gene/AFP/Getty Images; p. 30 © Dinodia/The Image Works; p. 32 Joe McNally/Getty Images; p. 36 Courtesy of Smith & Nephew, Inc.; p. 37 © Alfred Pasieka/Photo Researchers, Inc.; p. 38 Liu Jin/AFP/Getty Images.

**Designer:** Tahara Anderson; **Editor:** Kathy Kuhtz Campbell
**Photo Researcher:** Cindy Reiman